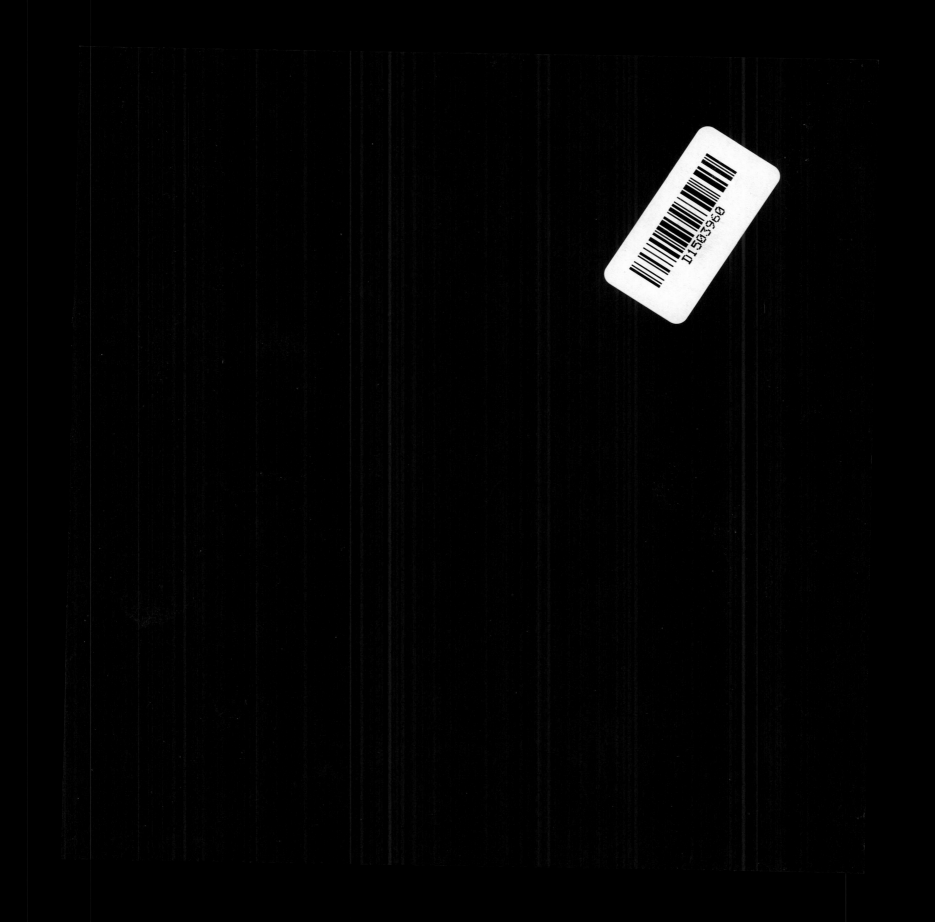

ZOMBIES

Aaron Frisch

CREATIVE EDUCATION

Published by Creative Education
P.O. Box 227, Mankato, Minnesota 56002
Creative Education is an imprint of
The Creative Company
www.thecreativecompany.us

Design and production by
Christine Vanderbeek
Art direction by **Rita Marshall**
Printed in the United States of America

Photographs by Alamy (AF Archive,
Gina Kelly, Moviestore Collection Ltd),
Getty Images (crisserbug, Renee Keith),
iStockphoto (Ivan Bliznetsov, Diane
Diederich, Grafissimo, Ralf Hettler,
Skip O'Donnell, becky rockwood),
Shutterstock (Tereshchenko Dmitry,
Germany Feng, Mikhail), Veer (James
Griehaber, Richard Kegler)

Library of Congress
Cataloging-in-Publication Data
Frisch, Aaron.
Zombies / Aaron Frisch.
p. cm. — (That's spooky!)
Includes bibliographical references
and index.
Summary: A basic but fun exploration
of zombies—dead bodies that rise from
the grave—including how they come to
exist, their weaknesses, and memorable
examples from pop culture.
ISBN 978-1-60818-251-0
1. Zombies—Juvenile literature. I. Title.

GR830.Z65F75 2013
398.21—dc23   2011051183

CPSIA: 070813 PO1714
9 8 7 6 5 4 3 2

CONTENTS

IMAGINE ...

You are walking past a **CEMETERY** at night. You hear the sound of dirt moving. Then you see a hand poke out of the ground. Suddenly, dead people are standing up and coming toward you!

ZOMBIES!

THAT'S SPOOKY!

WHAT IS A ZOMBIE?

A zombie is a dead person that can walk
around. Zombies wear normal clothes
like shirts or dresses. But zombies look
dirty and bloody from crawling out of the
ground. Zombies can be men, women, or
even kids.

A zombie's clothes quickly become dirty and torn

BECOMING A ZOMBIE

Sometimes a **CURSE** or **VIRUS** turns dead people into zombies. A person who gets bitten by a zombie might turn into one. A lot of times, no one knows why zombies come out of the ground!

People sometimes call zombies "the undead"

ZOMBIE BEHAVIOR

A zombie wants to eat people. It especially wants brains! A zombie cannot think. All it can do is see living people and then try to catch them. Most zombies can't talk. They just make moaning sounds.

The main thing zombies want is fresh brains

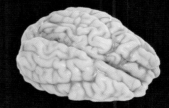

A Zombie's Powers

A zombie does not have any special powers. It may be easy to get away from one zombie. But zombies usually move in groups. They never get tired of chasing people.

Zombies attack only living people, not each other

A Zombie's Weaknesses

Most zombies are slow. They have stiff legs and arms. To stop a zombie, you have to kill it. This is hard, because zombies are already dead! People usually stop zombies by hitting or shooting them in the head. It is gross work!

A stick or bat can be handy when zombies are around

FAMOUS ZOMBIES

A scary movie called *Night of the Living Dead* is about zombies. They trap people in a farmhouse. In some newer movies, zombies are even spookier because they can run fast.

Night of the Living Dead scared moviegoers in 1968

Singer Michael Jackson made a famous **MUSIC VIDEO** for a song called "Thriller." In the video, zombies dance around! There are many video games with zombies. You might have to run from the zombies or shoot them.

Michael Jackson and his "Thriller" zombies (above)

LOOK FOR ZOMBIE FOOD

Zombies are not real. They exist only in movies and scary stories. But acting like a zombie can be fun. Put on some old clothes and roll around in dirt. Then walk around slowly and say, "Brains! BRAINS!"

To be a zombie, try to move stiffly and look hungry

THAT'S SPOOKY!

LEARN TO SPOT A ZOMBIE

wrinkled clothes

yellowish skin

bloody mouth

clawed, dirty fingers

DICTIONARY

CEMETERY a place where dead people are buried

CURSE a kind of magic spell that does something bad to a person

MUSIC VIDEO a very short movie that is set to a song

VIRUS a tiny living thing that can get inside people's bodies and make them sick

ZOMBIES

READ MORE

Hamilton, S. L. *Zombies*. Edina, Minn.: Abdo, 2011.

Pipe, Jim. *Zombies*. New York: Bearport, 2007.

Schuh, Mari C., and Aaron Sautter. *Zombies*. Mankato, Minn.: Capstone, 2007.

WEB SITES

ACTIVITY QUEST: ZOMBIE TAG

http://www.activityquest.com/activities/how-to-play-zombie-tag

This site tells you how to play a game called zombie tag.

FUNSCHOOL: HALLOWEEN

http://funschool.kaboose.com/fun-blaster/halloween/

This site has a lot of spooky games and pictures for coloring.

INDEX

becoming a zombie **8**

brains **11, 20**

cemeteries **4**

clothes **7, 20, 22**

curses **8**

movement **15, 16**

movies **16, 20**

stopping a zombie **15**

stories **20**

"Thriller" music video **19**

video games **19**

viruses **8**